pv   121794.   9.95 14.95
              7.95 Signed
              6.95
              5.95
              4.95

D0556151

OTHER BOOKS BY RON PADGETT

Poetry

Sweet Pea
Crazy Compositions
Tone Arm
Arrive by Pullman, with collages by George Schneeman
Grosse Feuerbälle
Tulsa Kid
Toujours l'amour
Triangles in the Afternoon
How to Be a Woodpecker, with drawings by Trevor Winkfield

Prose

Two Stories for Andy Warhol
How to Be Modern Art, with drawings by Trevor Winkfield
Among the Blacks

Collaborations

Bean Spasms, with Ted Berrigan
The Adventures of Mr and Mrs Jim and Ron, with Jim Dine
Antlers in the Treetops, with Tom Veitch
Oo la la, with Jim Dine

Translations

Some Bombs by Pierre Reverdy
The Poet Assassinated and Other Stories by Guillaume Apollinaire
Dialogues with Marcel Duchamp by Pierre Cabanne
Kodak by Blaise Cendrars
The Poems of A. O. Barnabooth by Valery Larbaud, with Bill Zavatsky

Books Edited

An Anthology of New York Poets, with David Shapiro
The Whole Word Catalogue 2, with Bill Zavatsky
The Point: Where Teaching & Writing Intersect, with Nancy Larson Shapiro
The Complete Poems of Edwin Denby
Handbook of Poetic Forms

Great Balls of Fire

POEMS BY RON PADGETT

For Randy

A fellow victim

of Poetry,

my best,

Ron Padgett

COFFEE HOUSE PRESS :: MINNEAPOLIS :: 1990

The publisher thanks the following organizations for their support of
this book: Dayton Hudson Foundation; Cowles Media/Star Tribune;
Northwest Area Foundation; and United Arts.

Coffee House Press books are distributed to trade by CONSORTIUM
BOOK SALES AND DISTRIBUTION, 287 East Sixth Street, Suite 365, Saint
Paul, Minnesota 55101. Our books are also available through all major
library distributors and jobbers, and through most small press dis-
tributors, including Bookpeople, Bookslinger, Inland, Pacific Pipe-
line, and Small Press Distribution. For personal orders, catalogs or
other information, write to:
COFFEE HOUSE PRESS
27 NORTH FOURTH STREET, SUITE 400, MINNEAPOLIS, MN 55401.

Library of Congress Cataloging in Publication Data

Padgett, Ron
Great balls of fire / Ron Padgett. — Rev. ed., rev., 2nd ed.
p. cm.
ISBN 0-918273-80-3 : $8.95
    I. Title.
PS3566.A32G7 1990   90-2457
811'.54 — dc20   CIP

9 8 7 6 5 4 3 2

Contents

To Patty and Wayne

GREAT BALLS OF FIRE

Detach, Invading

Oh humming all and
Then a something from above came rooting
And tooting onto the sprayers
Profaning in the console morning
Of the pointing afternoon
Back to dawn by police word to sprinkle it
Over the lotions that ever change
On locks
Of German, room, and perforate
To sprinkle I say
On the grinding slot of rye
And the bandage that falls down
On the slots as they exude their gas
And the rabbit lingers that pushes it

To blot the lumber
Like a gradually hard mode
All bring and forehead in the starry grab
That pulverizes
And its slivers
Off bending down the thrown gulp
In funny threes
So the old fat flies toward the brain
And a dent on brilliance

The large pig at which the intense cones beat
Wishes O you and O me
O cough release! a rosy bar
Whose mist rarifies even the strokers
Where to go
Strapping, apricot

After Reverdy

I would never have wanted to see your sad face again
Your cheeks and your windy hair
I went all across the country
Under this humid woodpecker
Day and night
Under the sun and the rain

Now we are face to face again
What does one say to my face

Once I rested up against a tree
So long
I got stuck to it
That kind of love is terrible

Nothing in That Drawer

Nothing in that drawer.
Nothing in that drawer.
Nothing in that drawer.
Nothing in that drawer.
Nothing in that drawer.
Nothing in that drawer.
Nothing in that drawer.
Nothing in that drawer.
Nothing in that drawer.
Nothing in that drawer.
Nothing in that drawer.
Nothing in that drawer.
Nothing in that drawer.
Nothing in that drawer.

Body English

Say something about still life.
At daybreak the sun rises—
Read out its highfalutin mess
Which is terror to the idiot
And the non-idiot alike, cut into
As we are on our trip to the water construction
Whose finish is a somersault
Done by a dark and angry rabbit.
But we listen with a valve open
Occupied with magnetic stacks
The blabbermouth responds to.
For it takes nerve to beat one's self
About the jaws—it takes, in fact,
Like a sudden phooey! illumination!
The thought centers shoot out
Through doors that open
Onto hideous lovers. . . .
The detective comes into all this
And goes to sleep. Lamps go
By in the night a dress brought.

The beak that discolors the apple
The teacher imagines
Is the same that reads your letters on the sly
Only to find that they were
Pecked out by a canary,
One shooting downward.

Shooting and cussing are pleasures
Ripped from the loudest
Lawyer in the world you call Casanova,
He whose rump is tickled by a tie
Riddled with buckshot.
Which brings me to guns:
There is a gun in this world—one
Limb is glue, the other tree—

That makes us all philosophers on seats,
Hateful tendency!
It's true we use our muscles
Being friendly
But at the same time we clear the range.
One thinks of the world as a hungry bird
Where fingers fly making a thing go.
Another applauds from his saddle
And rakes in the ancient chips
Father and brother knew.
It's Hallowe'en, was.

*

At least a pie is resting
On an ink pad. A pianist weeps
And jumps up. A confession is
Paddling its way up on high
Where he can't stand up. It grips him.
A button sails coolly toward his coward.
Who fails again!

But these vitamins that issue
From the back pocket covered with flowers
Cause a modest applause,
Yes ha ha!
One in a bottle that flies to a cripple—
Him and a gnat's bristle
Topping the mad alive book!

Pulling and straining,
You went out into the wrong snow
To measure like a mad fool.
Matches flare in the crevices

According to law
And die.
A snob in a skirt rolls past.

The panorama, which is growing truly vast,
Now reveals the lowest kind of person
And his peculiar trained weakness:
Adios. A detective comes in
And goes to sleep. He is
Unique.

Except at Night

Seurat and Gris do meet
Walking down the street.
How do you do, Seurat,
Says Gris, and How do you do,
Says Seurat, too.

A Careless Ape

The real reason I'm not you

Gillyflowers   Buttercups   Black-Eyed Susan

Is that I don't have your parts

                    plus some other little white buggers

However, we are friends

              My God!   My God!

And this is good

Mallarmé was a careless ape
In the writing of his work *Un Coup de dés*

Sunshine   pages   ziggedy black and red ants locked in mortal combat

He unwittingly made some letters and words   larger than others
Francis Ponge Fresca and Wayne
Emerge from a pasteboard box with their hands held high

              and placed them at enlarged parts of the pages

        very strange

202 CALO
DOG FOOD

As I said before I'm in pretty poor shape

Someone   a bee   a baby   a can of food

                         is screaming at me

We are so stupid we do not even know this

                                        This, I guess,
is my abiding problem
                         Others more transient swoosh by

It's a stupendously terrifying huge grotesque Flower Dog

        knocked out all night   through mist and rain
knocking my head softly against the bed weeping and crying

                                        Madonna!

Wayne you're a sweet boy   if only
How can we arrange everything so that everything is great?
If only we could all live in contentment   as you do
Some of the time

                              Unlike you
                 we live in perpetual torment and pain

                                        Are you okay?

I am not only okay I'm in perfectly stupendous shape

In fact

I am the excellent Alfred North Whitehead

buveur de l'opium chaste et doux

Drawn aside like music to show the notes glittering quietly below

16 November 1964

As this morning seemed special when I woke up
I decided, as is my custom, to go for a refreshing walk
In the street. Preparing myself for the unexpected, I
Combed my hair and generally made ready. I was ready.
In the hall outside my door the lady from down the hall
Shouted my name to get my attention. I waited
As she came down the hall with a newspaper in her hand.
I expected the worst. On the other hand, one can never tell
What mystery might spring up from the most commonplace,
For example, the lady and her newspaper. She wanted
To show me a headline which must have disturbed her,
Because her hands trembled as she read to me, "FIREMEN CHOP
THEIR WAY THROUGH SHED." I thanked the lady
And started toward the stairs when I realized that
The headline she had read me was rather astonishing.
I went back inside and wrote it down. Then down

In the street a suspicious-looking fellow approached me
And gave me a handbill, which, had not one of its words
Caught my eye, would have been quickly disposed of.
The word was "they"; it appeared once in the sentence,
"Do you realize that *they* are undermining your existence?"
I was puzzled by the fact that the word *they* should be italicized,
And the more I thought about it, the more it fascinated me.
Now, I have a small blue notebook which I carry with me
At all times, in case of any emergencies,
Such as the one I have just mentioned. I opened my book
To "T" and wrote down the word.
Well, my walk hadn't gotten along very far until
I remembered how close to the park I live, and how rarely
I go there. So picking up my stride and finally passing
A handsome girl, I reached the stone wall which bounds the park.
Ah, the red park! Where as a child I remember I had
Done so many things . . . . But that was in the dim past . . . .
Right in the middle of my reveries I felt someone
Looking at me and, turning, I was face to face with a very old man.

Who, without saying one word, gave me a small white card
With hands on it. Underneath the rows of hands
The card read: "I AM A DEAF MUTE. I SELL THIS CARD TO
    MAKE A LIVING. COULD YOU HELP? THANK YOU."
The old man did not take his eyes
Off me as I fished around in my pocket, and even after
I had dropped some coins into his limp hand, he stood there
Looking at me. How embarrassing it is when someone watches you
Put your hand into your pocket!
The old man finally shuffled away with my second donation.
I don't know why, but I was so upset that I had to sit down.
I disregarded the rain that never seemed to go away
From that bench, because I was so upset. A few moments
Later my senses came back to me and I found a small white card
In my hands, and its curious rows. Then I remembered
That their language is called "finger talk." The thought
Of talking fingers, so to speak, so thrilled me that the words
"Finger talk" went into my notebook, under "they." "Who knows,"
I said to myself, "by the end of the day I may have written a poem!"
"Now is no time to worry about poetry," my stomach chided me,
And I made my way out of the park, generally enjoying the air.

At one of the numerous lunch counters which dot our city
I ordered my lunch. The place was busy with people in a hurry,
And I knew I would have to wait for my order to arrive, and then
It would probably be the wrong thing or cold. To pass the time
I glanced through the two-page menu, which bore
On the title page the word "MENU."
Then it was that what had been happening to me all day,
This sudden illumination of the trivial, happened again.
Menu! How mundane, yet how miraculous! I wrote it down,
Under "M." It made my fourth entry, and I hoped for many more,
Since I have a great desire to write a long, beautiful poem,
Though I have nothing against short poems. But sometimes
I feel as if short poems are sort of a hoax, don't you?
Well, to get on, I finished the lunch, which was not
So bad as I had anticipated, and I once again met the air

With a light step. My next step? Who knows! I was full of vim! Vinegar!

It so happened that a young mother was strolling her little daughter
And that a small book dropped from the mother's handbag.
I went to fetch the book with every intention of returning
It to its proper owner, when I noticed the title and began
To think about it. The title was "THE PLUM, THE PRUNE, AND
     THE APRICOT."
Had this story once held me enchanted as a child? The last
Sentence seemed so familiar: "Forbidden pleasures leave a bitter taste."
It was all I could do to keep myself from bursting into tears,
And only the thought of recording this sentence, so mysterious
In its familiarity, prevented me from doing just that.
I slipped the book into my pocket, like a long-lost memento.
The experiences of this day, so exciting and wonderful, were still
Rather tiring, so I went into a theater to see a movie and to rest
My eyes. The movie was very boring and I soon left.
Back in my apartment I managed a small dinner, in. "TV DINNER."
Began to attract me, but when I went to write it down I hesitated:
The modern poet must be discriminating.

So now I sit in the kitchen writing in you, diary, a soda bottle
In my hand. "You are like me, soda bottle," I just said,
Shaking it and making it fizz. There must be something in a soda bottle
That we can understand, though I don't know what. Just as there must be
Something of value, to someone, in my blue notebook. I open my book
To see the four lines I have written down during the day, in those spare
    moments of inspiration:

    This offers us the stale air of the balcony
    Of the future which you don't want or can,
    Blue, marigolds, the sum of all that you love in him,
    Where is it?

Birches

When I see birches
I think of nothing
But when I see a girl
Throw away her hair and brains
I think of birches and I see them
One could do worse than see birches

Some Bombs

after Reverdy

1

One goes by like some oafs
On the K way the laminators along gents and lays you
The wagon turns on the roulette melee

Hair knights dress themselves in night
Moats which go by fount brutes

I ray you stop me pour the garter outdoors
Aw fond eel you all a quill train which darts
I ray you whar's sedans
Latrine key imports news and is Mobile in the vent

On intends

On Intends Creek
-cest a "whyso?" of the newt
The montage swallows a toot
Twos "suh" key oinks purrs the butt
Gene Autry sleeps

I'll send the Lautréamont coat, "Do, Monday
Awnglish Dan's a true key at the frond paws
One east tents with sin alley-oop
The sill is fond

And a pea-tit galosh dresses itself oh bored Walter by the sea

2

I'll nudge sir the mount blank
And one goose clock son sedans

Josquin has a procession of gins in black Dis End

The curs broil a neck-green few
A mince hombre author of *Sack Cur*
Says Monty Martyr
The lune foams a quintet
Rondeau comes your figure

O tempts these flames plus Ardennes
And Desnos jures
Shack a petty toilet
They ramps
Lash Larue is black and the sill Clare

A sullen hominy veils the hut
Analogues robe Blanche
The loaned hand is a dim haunch

One sort of that maize sends vocabulary
One is gay
A bomb ear trembles in core of the knee

The plus Grant champ do mowed is in reverse
And debates coo her
Elves divulge and plow Sir Key who is past saying
The ensign manacle eats depasturized

Fund of the hombre you remoo
At home Monty tits anew
The solenoid saps you he on his hilt
Caws "one Sulla quoit pus commerce fit"

Me nudity

A home marches the suit and divan
The sane is la-la
And one intends on the Oh to clack paws
The rest sea pass Dan the rest turret Donne you we

3

The pied quarts of Chevrolets trim blent Sir her eyes on
The memo leg's knee asserts me with coo
Monday is a tent soused with covered fur
The fen beings brillo like the years

One of the arms pour rear
And a cur pours more rear

The General et an old monster
Sand's civil habits
A Black blight a bone Blake blight at the fair
Ah a member of the fame isle
Says Louie Key a prissy toot he row is my parasol

The cur is a pre-sound without a rage where Lou too urns without fins

Blue as a hurry
Monty "The Soup" Godzilla
His figuring is a Negro Roy decorated with my soft age

He purrs Rye Anne

Chase the salvages
The music mews
New sums try and I sew O mildew
Where's Alley Ooops
The plays here ate Mort author of *News*

4

Isle yards means Key peasant
Kill cue chose the pass in the vent
Troy's tea (rooftop) teas De Moins ballerina cent
Malasia par tint I found D train
Your river pace attempts
May's a pong my sentiment

A man is a tomb
Kill coon sort of ate Nesbit's rent tree
O sank he him the lamb pest is two juries halloo May

Dance the newt
Souse the P. Louie
Ate 10 franks do tax he

The numerous tom bee "hallo"

El Paso invents the bush of gout
The tru
Kill gout
The pen drool key bat dances the maize on is come a cur
The isle has dice monuments where Lon foods rat et her milly hair
"Ew!" to hear kill coon

There now there's a pig

A no ear chat files on Sir Nigeria

And desk chins!
This chins Cousin Crane's minds less a gents

La looney is fat I guess of gartering the newt
Ellie is a party
And I vase my meter
"The portie no me suitee dee rainee nor the fen beings!"

I pry pour and moo the con's sea urge do, by Dis
Celery you too vice
Blah hurries won bash floor
Don's lovie I am Surrey I am Tojo ours levee bastard

The temperature was basted
I neighed "Run fast"

An hombre glistened in tree cur ate your din
I Surrey lying in Kore demand matin'

Sir the trot tore
Desk vice ages flow tent ah bass dance the drooly yard

5

My dog sag knee
Jet Chris
A Vic
Lee rig knee of old Roys is finite
The rivets is a jam bone
Lewd
Key pinned play fond
Ate the sender of ton cigars
Continent toot the loom hair

O day two our do shimmy
Less armrests sign it
The solenoid ass askin'
In 's England lispins
And cooks "keep off" Dan's the priory who meed

The sore where indoor mitt the prim hair chat haunt
Epee ivory
Mess mine rests moose pen dent la
And the "See Hell" may soot ten
See Hell lava mess yours toots the matins

Ma man roughest on mot-
An apple breath pal pits sang a lot
Do sang "Versailles the Paper Boulevard"
Lucre nekkid rye hen

March the attachés' gizzard does Mary
Enter Rousseau noise key vaunt flues loin
A bout Monday where Lon mat tin
Brezska fought any or less gouts he sang key coo lent of moan cur which
        Lon Rin Tin
A clay iron dances as sure sonny la gin rail

6

Lee bid on the pet role
And the brute
Celery kill the party writ

A marionette skin till
Dance the newt

The tramp way tray (rooftop) ee you knee my load I dance sez Ruse
Ate a Chevrolet the loom hair
The utensils sell key passes by the party hair
Sez jukes are tombs sit the ray isle
You'n rat faculty tiff purse honey Dis skinned
A rampart
They trey in my cur ate messmates see sore tson ten retarred

I food raise for ire the boot detest soul ears
I food raise salve rays sick of two pence decept reamer boy age Gene
        Autry
Their hair the Autrys

Isles send Von invite. Ills taunt lazy
Acorn do trot tore
Ate the puppy key sordid a foe is decibel
Dance the fit rind
Tea did it bounce sore

Lash Larue is Rio Grande and Tristan comma a bully fardle

Words to Joe Ceravolo

I think tonight I am beginning to understand some impulses
That a friend of mine Joe Ceravolo seems to have been having
And which others have certainly had
Which makes no difference
But which might make him seem terribly silly for a while
And which if I'm right I'm beginning to feel myself
About now and therefore sympathize with
It's a cheap sympathy when you have to come about it like this
But who cares

Listen, Joe Ceravolo
You're O.K.

Falling in Love in Spain or Mexico

A handsome young man and a veiled woman enter. They stroll slowly across the stage, pausing from time to time, so that their entrance coincides with the first spoken word and their exit the last.

JOSE: I am happy to meet you. My name is José Gomez Carillo. What is your name? This is my wife. I like your daughter very much. I think your sister is beautiful. Are you familiar with the U.S.? Have you been to New York? Your city is very interesting. I think so. I don't think so. Here is a picture of my wife. Your daughter is very beautiful. She sings very well. You dance very well. Do you speak English? Do you like American movies? Do you read books in English? Do you like to swim? To drive a car? To play tennis? Golf? Dance? Do you like American music? May I invite you to dance? I like to play tennis. Will you drive? Do you live here? What is your address? Your phone number? I am here for four days. Two weeks. One month only. Would you like a cigarette? A glass of wine? Anything? Help yourself. To your health! With best regards. Many happy returns! Congratulations! With best wishes! Merry Christmas! My sincere sympathy. Good luck! When can I see you again? I think you are beautiful. I like you very much. Do you like me? May I see you tomorrow? May I see you this evening? Here is a present for you. I love you. Will you marry me?

GIRL: *(She lifts and throws back her veil, revealing her face, which is extraordinarily beautiful.)* Yes!

THE END

Autumn's Day

Rilke walks toward a dime. I saw.
It was very great. But now
His shadow is fast upon the sundials.
How then can the winds remind
The shadows it is late?

"Who has no home cannot build now,"
Said Rilke to a grasshopper.

Little grasshopper,
You must waken, read, write long letters, and
Wander restlessly when leaves are blown.

Y . . r D . . k

It w.s c....h f.r t..m to go b..k to t.e h...e
T..y h.d r..d a...t it

I am s.....g d..n to w...e y.u
A...t t..s a.d a...t b....e he d..d
He l...s on h.s o.n f....r a.d s.n

It t..k f..r of t..m to c...y in t.e s......s
F..m t.e s...l s..t g...n p..d
T.e c....g w.s t......e

T.e i.e c..e w..n he w.s w.....g f.r it

It c.....s i....f n..t me
C....g b..k t.....h t.e g....d
D....y c........s
B...k p..e of w.....g
S...e t...e is n.....g b.......l in t.e w.y

T.o w..n f...r w.s c......g t.e w...e
t..t d..t t..t m....r
N.t to c..e b..k w.....d a.d s...n in a s...y

V......e a...e in t.h d........g
O..e u........d we d.......d
T....h it g...s no p......e as d..s w.....r

On t.e s....l b......n b...d
L....s a..........g in t.e h...s
T.e t...g we i........d as a b....e
Or t.o f....s of r.d in t.e t...s
(He w.s w.....g to it)

C.n be k..t in p.....s a.d n.t d.......d k..p
G...g o.f a.y m....t
K..p t..m o.f

To k..p in m..d on a p...h d...g t.e r..n?
No m..e t..n o.....g o...s y....r h..d to l...h
No m..e o.......e to it t..n to a b...n d.g

Poulain

An orange and blue box of Poulain chocolate
Is what I think of often
As I sit just outside the late afternoon sunlight—
I see it in another light
Sitting on a brown oak or something table,
Maybe a white kitchen one,
And when I reach out for it
My hand touches it
And I pick it up

Mister Horse

Mmmm
I get up and am seized by the present
Whose presence is
As a roof fits on a house whose car in the garage
Backs out
And in the back seat
Childhood is normal but the scaffolding thrown up around
The road is built with an insane logic
Which is at once its interest and its uselessness
Save as torment

Not an example is a loose nail here
One I caught my sleeve on
But I've moved
Up to the floor all in blue
And the décor is stunning in its vacuity
As if the air were suddenly sucked out
By a passing machine
The one we ride and operate
With our hands and feet

So the landscape turns out to be a dial
Of stars and numbers
No less fascinating than the cold pair of scissors
That cut the shirt you are now wearing
The starry one of water
In the quickly deflating evening

Evening is so small these days
It's the size of a green pea
The small expensive kind
That come in a silver can
That rolls for a long time
Decorated with a fleur-de-lis

Which is the sole bud in the sky at the moment

Other times
You'd have the flower in your buttonhole
Its center round and packed with goodness
Like the yellow of a sunny-side up egg

But the egg is exempt
From nature's clumsy machinery
It is something very much like your own heart
A lady drops on the way home
On the sidewalk in some small town in Arizona
Where it fries secretly
And is then whisked away by a tumbleweed
Or eaten by a horse
The same one I feel as if I mentioned a moment ago

I would like to devote my special attention
To this horse
Let me tell you about it
It can jump a bush a small one
It is the kindest horse in the world
That is why it is the subject of so many thoughts
That is why it bites both the apple and you
And why when the blinders are put on
It weeps

And with good reason!
For now it is a mere piece of glossy paper
The only furniture in this room
Whose blue it takes on
And whose flower has gone a terrible green
Under the influence of the hard light
Whose manipulations increase
In proportion to the scales they're laid against

Yes, I'm afraid today's just a chart
Plowing through a stormy sea
But the horse is still here!
He's at F-3
And is marked with a blue and green dot
The green a concession to the plant world

Whose proper domain
Is growing on the living
This sort of radiant fungus
You noticed in the last picture I sent you

I didn't think you'd see it
Since the photograph was not of me even
Though at first my thoughts filled it with me
I sent it as a compensation
For the money I owe you
And whose astonishing presence neither
Of us will ever really know
We have been short-changed by the modern world
But at least we got our receipt

Maybe we'd better keep it
Since nature is so expensive
And day pops up like a big number inside a cash register
Perhaps I'd better forget about the forest and the hills
And the balls that lie there covered with pins

These are the same pins I stuck in you
To wish you a speedy recovery
And to hint that you need no longer pursue the rain
With your magnificent intelligence
Which is sparkling and fizzing loudly
Across these many years to me

But now I really must be going
The horse is getting restless and no wonder
I only gave him a piece of paper to eat today
By the way
He's just a mule
But I don't think that will make any difference
To him in the long run
Also I hope that you won't mind
If I send him to visit you sometime

Homage to Max Jacob

Goodbye sting and all my columbines
In the tower which looks out gently
Their yo-yo plumage on the cold bomb shoulder
        Goodbye sting.

Goodbye house and its little blue roofs
Where such a friend in all seasons
To see us again made some money
        Goodbye house.

Goodbye line of hay in pigs
Near the clock! O! how often I hurt myself
That you know me like an apartment
        Goodbye line!

Goodbye lamb grease! hands carrying arteries
On the well varnished little park mirror
Of white barricades the color of diapers
        Goodbye lamb grease!

Goodbye verges calves and planks
And on the sting of our black flying boat
Our servant with her white hair-do
        Goodbye verges.

Goodbye my clear oval river
Goodbye mountain! Goodbye cherry trees!
It is you who are my cap and tale
        Not Paris.

Wind

Now it is over and everyone knew it
The bad grass surrendered in unison and with much emotion
The long-awaited became despised
Everyone got tired and concluded that phase

Reports followed, causing intrusions
In the old-timers. Others go off for refreshment
The distrustful student prefers German popular songs
A language he does not understand

But now there is the tremendous reassurance of being
At the dinner table and tense, a stalwart melody
Tromping to its fluorescent conclusion.
This you find unimaginable, that rent should be suddenly so high
Up there in the cupola, the gauze
The tiny excitement of the generator
The note you read without even looking at it
Going back where you lose your hands you bask
Whitewash vistas a voice that finally remembers
Hedges that were once formidable
You watch and are horrified to be a part of it

The booth puts you out for miles this speedometer
The "fertile lowlands" you chalk it up in orange
And again a brush applies the proper lascivious colors
The postcard making it "right" instead of wrong

The Blind Dog of Venice

The tartar sauce lesson was misunderstood
By those who didn't even want to miss it.
Just in the nick of time the knob came forth with kleenex,
The cow licked its way into our foreheads.
We responded with great tonsils, though we were soon
To forget that the angel of logic
Is not logic, and that the power of a personal
Hair is more aware than unusual.
This was the choir boy's dead.
Everyone moved up a row.

Later you beat me to a pulp magazine
Which I desired most fiercely, in thus wise
To far errands o'er the earth.
In the domino stand we committed the sin of homework
To drift up against the door and dream
Of a dog who would dream of a circle which draws a dream around us
Then your long, leather smile consoled me
As far as the potbellied stove, in which had been placed
Our name, address, and age.
The delivery boy turned away from the door in despair,
His a fruitful mission!

What could we have been left out of?
Did it fall among the positive dominos? A vicious
Song leaped out of the frying pan.
The result is more high and low Latin, these letters
I am getting to and from you through our new past, since now
The mist is getting bigger
Over the sarsaparilla-colored pond and the searchlights
Which are getting cut down through the trees
Reveal the gentleman lawn reclining in a gesture of crassness.

The Ems Dispatch

Opening up a mud duck
The sin of the hearth had made him handsome
Don't ever give me what continues to be the tan arm of the hero
As identical, these sums and the chance to disappear
By including the chamois
Though that's a fine mess, I wist
Titles, etc.   2. Two Veins.   followed, pursued, sought after
But the curse now
Laid you down in the patient tent
Where there are men, there are no men
Just what I wanted (lie) perfect (lie)
I cared for the boy's drawing of the horse to get going
Then the lovely shin quest
Into the untracked signal gun, flowers, birthdays, sonnets
Put the hot, sweet breath of your breath against mine enemy
Come with me the nurse ferocity
Streets streets and less equal streets
The sails being torn to pieces in the upstairs part
But in a few moments
Without themes space or the invisible table message
Under the legs "far" into the night our hut
Its flaming gates
And the invitation to commit bibliography
The proffered hand
Guessed we're on to each other
The lice looked up in astonishment
Didn't explain the available cardboard murder
Going on into the mail covered with rust and the box
The great shoe prediction sigh clock
No doubt about it the neighbor thought it over
The extra put on its countenance and clicked on off
Let my dog sleep
On the altar of girlhood
But polish around it, observing the priority of the bump
The close call packed away and sniffing at the edge

The Life of M.

"The true test of a man is a bunt. So kiss me!
O please come back to me! Then go away . . .
I only like you for a long time.
And then: "The gaucho is coming!"

The old room back in you
Or a complicated object by a pond
Weren't exactly "piled up"
But a tall short masculine kept starting to go

There's nothing in this box
Or the one in it but what's there?
Brown old arithmetic, a stopwatch,
A wrist and some h.........n.
Put them back. They are good for you.

No! They aren't! For they still love
Though the toe has been
But off the bumper crop of fumes.
Besides, the gaucho is almost here.

I'd Give You My Seat If I Were Here

The shadows these flowers are making on each other
The wild and sleepy eyes they make
Are being thrown against the notion *de voyager*
By fingers that are not silver or blue and they point

This keeps happening for eleven months.
But tonight she's in her grave at the bottom of the sea,
Leaving us at that.

If I could tell you why
The delicious crunch of feathers
Through fifteen heads of yours
Can encourage and surround
Then there would be no need for this needle in my head
Or the electricity that is not really mine.

Though it is only real,
My dream to raise no curtain on the other stage
That isn't there, but there
Under the breeze of a handkerchief
That is brushing against the temple you will find
On either side of your head—

And you know and you know.

After the Broken Arm

From point A a wind is blowing to point B
Which is here, where the pebble is only a mountain.
If truly heaven and earth are out there
Why is that man waving his arms around,
Gesturing to the word *lightning* written on the clouds
That surround and disguise his feet?

If you say the right word in New York City
Nothing will happen in New York City;
But out in the fabulous dry horror of the West
A beautiful girl named Sibyl will burst
In by the open window breathless
And settle for an imaginary glass of something.
But now her name is no longer Sibyl—it's Herman,
Yearning for point B.

Dispatch this note to our hero at once.

A Man Saw a Ball of Gold

A man saw a ball of gold in the sky;
He climbed for it,
And eventually he achieved it—
It was gold.

Now this is the strange part:
When the man went to the earth
And looked again,
Lo, there was the ball of gold.
Now this is the strange part:
It was a ball of gold.
Ay, by the heavens, it was a ball of gold.

To Francis Sauf Que

I

You think of everything:
Modern silence, where I go back continually
To you, as does everyone, it seems . . . .

2

We are getting younger, perhaps

3

I "hate you hate you

4

The man walks under the house
In the Renaissance, the plum etc.

5

More data, adversity is like walking
In the sun which is shining on you
In bed, where you are with her,

"everything like that"

6

Now I love you again because of these roosters

7

Yours is topography to me in my dim head. I'm sorry, the virgins.

8

This color, orange, tries to remind me of you,
Orange slice

9

And you are

10

Sometimes I leaped at the wrong time
Or right time, this made you who shall receive
This scarlet rose with some sort of greatness happy

11

I thought so, so you changed your fasteners.
I think I hate you more than anyone else.

12

If only you knew how to ignore me

13

Then symbolism gets a model today,
But you didn't believe in that, its flaxen gray—
And neither does the porch
More than these worth taking notes on

14

I didn't hear you when you all did it

15

I will kill you

17

To envisage your doom (it), and,
"Get with it, kid"

18

To be plucked at exactly 2:10 in the morning

19

They faded en masse onto the yearbook,
The shoelace through six years of catatonia,
Of Gérard Labrunie and this

20

So whose shadow is this, yours or mine? and why
Are there two of us here instead?

When I Think More of My Own Future Than of Myself

Coming out of the bathroom
That one has to go down the stairs one-half flight
Out a door into an elevated courtyard
Along a little balcony to get to
I often have the thought
"How sad it is that I must die"

I do not think this thought proceeds
From emerging from the bathroom
Though emerging from the bathroom
Can change one's thoughts
—Just as, since my college studies,
When the thought was made available to me,
I have never been able to make any sort of really reasonable connection
Between Love and Death

The Complete Works

The big black bear and the prowling panther lived near our beautiful school
Irving received seven dollars for moving.
A rib hung from the marble bust of Robert Burns.
Alfred's friend lifted the tough fire.
Phyllis found the hand on the sofa.
Becky led the sob to the bakery.
Marian and Marvin were married in the month of May.
Maurice and Edmund tramped many miles over muddy rods.
Whittaker left the waffle under the wagon wheel.
Harvey proved that atomic particles are ugly.
Steve is suffering from severe oldness.
Mr. Thurston thwarted the plans of the three bugs.
The thirsty mouth took the broth and ran southward.
Ruthless Judy threw the red thimble through the door of the thatched
    cottage.
We criticized the wound and swatted it around.
They went bathing in the other broth.
Ruth saw a beautiful moth on the white sloth.
Toot! Toot! Thump! Thump! Theo is tooting the horn and Tim is
    thumping the table.
Tin is a soft, lustrous metal which becomes brittle when heard.
Edgar divided the dainties among the fiends.
Dick wept farther and further into the dense wood.
Then Dan did the daring deed.
Gilbert left his hat, coat, and foot in the boat.
The artist bought tiny paint.
Ottawa, the capital of Canada, is situated in Ontario on the Ottawa
    River.
Put these beans and peas on your back.
The thieves took Sylvia's vacation.
Baby's rubber ball bounced into the world.
Steve drove twelve snails into the sieve.
The fawn jumped the fence and found the forest.
Rufus put the rash into the refrigerator.
Strive to remove that vine from the shelves.
Rob tumbled from the ranch and fell into a berry.

Elizabeth and Alberta sobbed when they read *Black Beauty*.
Maples, hemlocks, and elms grew on Mr. Miller's forearms.
Martin promised mother he would come with Tom.
The wood was watching the woodcutter.
Mrs. Mather soothed the withered loaf.
The thoughtless teamster turned himself into Third Street.
Theodora placed the thick pimple on her thumb.
Martha took the wreath from her box.
Beth thought Ruth's fourth toot came through slowly.
The brothers cut the heat with a scythe.
Their mother gave each of them a fart.
Tom threw the thorny stick into Teddy's steak.
Did the bath save Fanny and her brothers?
Wilbert and Herbert walked to the tulip in the heart of the forest.
Mr. Dunn drove directly to the dent.
The timid deer turned his lifted head, gazed toward the meadow, and
     listened.
That cold December day Douglas waded through deep drifts to the drug
Then father placed Paul in the park.
We voted to remove evil and vice from the aged.
The visitor viewed the duck in the valley.
Frieda frightened the leaf by telephoning the officer.
Did the horse whinny when he neared the arf?
The wizard waved his wand underneath the weeping.
The servant left the shove on the walk.
Thelma and Theodore yanked the studious youth.
The author thought Nathan less and less.
But Kenneth found the heat in the path.
The silver scythe fell into the seething pool.
Moths gathered on their fathers.
The northern weather was severed.
Dawson made a pond for the ducks by damaging a ditch.
That day they drove the north wind into town.
The maiden found the plant trodding its way into the ground.
The stick was sighted near the table.
Three silver thumbs stood there on the shelf.
A red cross stepped from the bus and entered the hospital.
St. Augustine is the coldest man in the United States.
Later the valet put five cravats into the waltz.

Mr. Porter presented the diplomas to the pups.
The wee whistler wailed when he was wheeled away.
Mr. Nicholson and Lester saw the works at Syracuse.
John gave ten dimes for the meat and nine cents for the meat
We saw the month on Theodor's new spring suit.
Did the frogs leap, thus making rips on the pond?
The Arab beckoned the man to the cur.
Walter wheeled the wheelbarrow full of wild followers.
Columbus sailed away from pain.
The snowmen looked at pictures from their frozen youth.
Jack jumped when he heard the huge gnat.
Julia washed the dish and put it on herself.
Brother and sister were hardening in the garden.
Robert Bruce learned the lesson of perversity from a spider.
Mrs. Moore will hire Mr. Ayre to imagine the sheep.
We could hear the roar more distinctly as we drew the shore.
Oranges and fruit grow in Florida.
Arnold knelt beside the vat of chili.
Did the careless driver puncture the corner store?
Harry likes breathing but Rebecca prefers Brussels.
Health is better than health.
The halleluja rejoiced at the hurrah.
The steam was leaking in the rain.
La Salle and his hand explored Louisiana.
Kenneth's curiosity caused him to kick the cake again.
The truck broke down and wept.
Cora's uncle took a picture of the country.
On Christmas Eve crawled down the chimney.
Thomas brushed his face.
The engine watched the huge machine crush the pebble.
Eliza sold six zuzu snaps to Ezra.
Lucretia wished to become an illusion.
The car crashed into the sandman and pushed him over.
Papa found a law in the umbrella.
Duncan was listening to the wrong nightingale.
Yes! Yes! shouted the mouth from the yacht.
Jim injured his wrist when he slapped the hill.
Emmet and Elliot enjoyed the mayor's chest.
Mrs. Swan gave Oliver a dollar for doing "odd" jobs.

A drop of ink dropped on the college.

The jacket ran along the bank.

The unusual seizure of the Parisian gown caused great confusion.

Richard tilted the merchant toward Mars.

The fragrance of sweet peas was wafted to the piazza.

Did the allusion to the event destroy the Hoosier's composure?

The Missouri River is a tribute to the Mississippi.

The tire felt better when it had rested.

Edward addressed the envelope with sharp tones.

But the man drank the brook and saved his son.

After dinner Pearl and her mother walked on their sweaters for two hours.

Rare, red raspberries grow in their raving.

The whistle was heard over the hustle and bustle of the meat.

The wealth dwelt in a belt.

Then on Saturday Grandpa planted the rash.

He said, "Sound the last in angel, mountain, and ruin."

So Henrietta had money for lunch.

Harvey and Horace hid the hammer in the cut.

The roof leaked and the boys were damaged.

Dick lugged the heavy leg to the doctor.

"Quack quack," said the duck to the quadruped.

Six pecks of history were in the bag.

The quiet had started in quest of the quail.

Leaning against the gate was a rag.

The courteous cloak called a cab for the colonel.

Soon we were to learn that Lucy and Rose were part apple.

The ex-clown thrust his throbbing thumb into the slave.

Clarice makes delicious ice.

Trailing vines and large trees, we grow in the tropics.

The South Atlantic Ocean is east of North America.

The wind piled up around our house.

Did Eleanor enter the boat and erase the farther shore?

On Wednesday Helen and Harry entertained an idea.

You fill out the yellow metal questionnaire.

Frank sang to the ground when he turned his ankle on the riverbank.

The youth longed to try his strength by swimming the length of his tan.

The sick musician made a quick rip in his physician.

The drugs weighed exactly ounces.

The carpenter fasted with screws.
Meanwhile Quentin inquired the whereabouts of the question.
The beggar thanked Nancy for the pun.
The heroine wore a satin dress and a coral neck.
Even so, in the spring wens come to this meadow.
The Eighteenth Amendment prohibits the selling of beverages.
Robert McDuffy gave his father away in a fit of generosity.
Eleanor Ross tossed the ball into the feces.
A gust of wind sent Ben's hat into lust.
That chair is upstairs in the bare room.
The toy child destroyed the adjoining room.
A tall boy stood up in the state of Montana.
A severe storm sent the vessel against the beep.
The lucid explanation subdued the ears of the multitude.
But Archibald argued with Harvey about the quality of the khaki arf.
The goose looked at the pillows in the brook.
Earl hurled the burning captain to the curb.
The literary cricket praised the poem.
One morning Claude saw a yawn walking alone by the wall.
Papa drove the car into the father.
The cadet saluted the Ten Commandments.
Nora saw a white organ in the window.
O it was terrible!
The hungry monkey finished off several nuts.
The brook ran on through Mr. Woolsey's food.
Look! Look! A pussy by the brook!
The organist laughed when the choir rebelled.
The three millennia then approached the bone.
Margaret gave the hungry god some meat.
The Wicks sent the box of wax to the monks by express.
The foreigner examined the ruined Latin.
Green moss and gray lichens grew on its old hoof.
Christopher laughed at the cranberries through the gate.
The eloquent lecturer requested the head to sing.
Listen to the restless wind in the Europeans.
At last at dusk the brisk skate returned.

Jet Plane

Flies across sky

Buckets

Of rain
hit the buildings
but we in our apartments
are kept dry by the buildings they're in

the rain is rolling off the buildings
and bouncing off
and the roofs keep the rain from getting us wet

the ceiling is not letting any water in

it goes spat spat spat
on the windowledge
trying to get in

the windowpane is streaked with rain
trying to come in

to go everywhere

to make everything wet

I am lying in my bed
head near the window

aware of all this
thinking How Great

We Win

You Again

I think I'm smoking too much too many cigarettes
And with a sore throat coming on why don't I
Get to bed watch a string
Of late movies there're some pretty good ones on
Tonight the apartment is colder than
Usual when it's usually verging on broiling   if I were
A lobster I wouldn't be getting a sore throat and certainly
Wouldn't be smoking and cigarettes are so high
In New York   an odd situation   in Vermont
I'm going to stop smoking even
Though I love to smoke like a
Turk in Tulsa the cigarettes are cheaper and Dick
Is smoking them up   pretty soon he'll be back
To enjoy the luxury of smoking as opposed to the habit
I ought to read Cendrars but
He makes me want to smoke and squint and hit
Someone in the heart as you've hit me
Every day this week and I'm glad I don't drink so there

Ode to the Astronauts

O astronauts!
You have flown higher than our dear Dante!
His light is as a flashlight to yours
That is the sun of our solar system!
The Arno was his to walk over
While to you it is less than a tear!
And while Virgil stands at the door
Moving his ugly fingers,
You are pushing the bright new shiny buttons of your machine!

Ode ai Astronauti/ O astronauti!/ Siete volati più in alto del nostro caro
Dante!/ La sua luce è come una lampadina tascabile di fronte alla tua/
Che è il sole del nostro sistema solare!/ L'Arno era il suo da attraversare/
Mentre per voi è meno d'una lacrima!/ E mentre Virgilio sosta alla
porta/ Movendosi le dita brutte/ Voi maneggiate le lucide maniglie della
vostra macchina!

Ode to the Futurist Painters and Poets

Futurist painters and poets!
You are finished!
The youth of modern Italy no longer listens to your horrible shrieks!
Marinetti, your *parole in libertà* were just a gibberish of stupid thinking!
Boccioni, you died young and we do not hate you, though we do not love
    you, either.
Papini, your Christ was recently buried in Milan under a heap of Fiats!
Gino Severini, you thought you were smart by living in Paris and
    associating with the Cubists, but you were only deceiving yourself
    and your fellows . . . .
I know you are dead and I weep
But that does not change your absurd notions of life and art!
You, Futurists, thought the airplane and telephone so wonderful! Ha!
Tomorrow an Italian will walk on the moon
And the day after, Italian youth will live on the sun—
O great flashlight! sun, greater than Dante's light or Boccaccio's
    flickering candle,
You shine down on the graves of those who are now dead forever, the
    Futurist painters and poets!

Ode ai Poeti e Pittori Futuristi/ Poeti e pittori futuristi!/ Voi siete finiti!/ La
gioventù dell'Italia non ascolta più le vostre grida orribili!/ Marinetti, le
tue *parole in libertà* erano soltanto balorde stupidità!/ Boccioni, tu sei morto
giovane e non ti odiamo anche se non ti vogliamo bene./ Papini, il tuo
Cristo è stato da poco sepolto a Milano sotto un mucchio di Fiat!/ Gino
Severini, tu ti credevi furbo recandoti a Parigi e legandoti ai cubisti, ma ti
ingannavi te stesso ed i tuoi colleghi e basta . . . ./ So che sei morto e
piango,/ Ma ciò non cambia le vostre assurde idee sulla vita e sull'arte!/
Voi, futuristi, credevate meraviglioso l'aeroplano e il telefono! Pah!/
Domani un italiano passeggerà sulla luna e l'indomani la gioventù
italiana si troverà sul sole—/ O grande lampadina tascabile! sole, più
grande della luce di Dante o della candela scintillante del Boccaccio,/ Tu
illumini le tombe di loro che ora sono morti per sempre, i poeti e pittori
futuristi!

Fiat Ode

Fiat!
You have freed us from our dusty dreadful past
In which Boccaccio,
Though he is often very funny,
Has kept us locked up in the old-fashioned rooms
Of his long *Decameron*!
Fiat! we ride in you
Past the graves of the early Tuscan lyric poets
Not even knowing where they are
And not even caring very much
Because they are dead!

Ode alla Fiat/ Fiat!/ Tu ci hai liberati dal nostro passato pauroso ed
antiquato,/ nel quale il Boccaccio,/ benchè spesso sia molto divertente,/
ci ha tenuti rinchiusi nelle camere antiquate del suo lungo *Decamerone*!/
Fiat! noi passeggiamo con voi/ davanti alle tombe dei dugentisti toscani/
non sapendo nemmeno dove essi siano/ e non curandoci poi gran che/
perchè essi siano morti!

Ode to Giuseppe Ungaretti

D.C. Italian sphinx semi-divine! fled from Egypt's sizzling figs in your
    nineteenth year!
To the banks of the Tiber
You, Giuseppe, have sat like a stupendous hoary battery these fifty years!
Sending forth energy from the electrode and anode of your nose!
You knew the fizzing terror of the First World War and the double terrors
    of the Second!
Literary movements you have—bah!—brushed them under your
    intelligence with a broom!
And they died of electrocution!
For you are greater than movements—or movement!
(Even though it was your pleasure to visit New York in 1965)
You did not leave us, you could not!
For you are covered with the olives of desire for Italy
Where the olive trees bend toward your boat as you return, as on a
    magnet!
The shoelaces of the boot come unlaced and reach out for you, Italy's
    greatest twentieth-century poet!

Ode a Giuseppe Ungaretti/ Sfinge italiana semi-divina di corrente diretta!
fuggito dai fichi scottanti d'Egitto a diciannove anni!/ Alle sponde del
Tevere/ Tu, Giuseppe, sei rimasto come una stupenda pila candida per
cinquant'anni!/ Emettendo l'energia dal anodo e dal eletrodo del tuo
naso!/ Tu conoscevi il terrore frizzante della prima guerra mondiale ed i
terrori raddoppiati della seconda!/ I movimenti letterari tu hai—pah!—
spazzati sotto la tua intelligenza con una scopa!/ E sono morti per
l'elettricità!/ Perchè tu sei più grande dei movimenti—del movimento
stesso!/ (Benchè sia stato il tuo desiderio di recarti a New York nel 1965)/
Non ci hai lasciati—non potevi!/ Perchè tu sei coperto degli ulivi di
desiderio per l'Italia/ dove gli ulivi si piegano verso la nave al tuo ritorno
come verso una calamita!/ I lacci dello stivale si slegano e si stendono a
te, il più grande poeta italiano del ventesimo secolo!

Ode to Mussolini

Mussolini, we do not want your brain in our country!
It reeks of the hateful Fascism of the '30s
And which still persists!
Though we respect your wife and understand her desire to have your
       complete remains,
We do not want it here!
The Smithsonian Institution in Washington
Is a better resting place
For the hideous gray contents of your skull!

Ode a Mussolini/ Mussolini, noi non vogliamo il tuo cervello nel nostro
Paese!/ Esso puzza del Fascio odioso degli anni trenta il che perdura
ancora!/ Anche se noi rispettiamo la tua moglie e capiamo il suo
desiderio di avere le tue spoglie intere,/ il tuo cervello non lo vogliamo
qui!/ All'Istituto Smithsonian di Washington troverà riposo migliore il
contenuto grigio e orrendo del tuo teschio!

The Sandwich Man

The funny thing is that he's reading a paper
As if with his throat
With the bottom half folded neatly under his chin
Which is, incidentally, clean-shaven
As he strolls absently toward us, toting a sewing machine
On the front
With delicate little gold lines curling and swaying below a white spool in
      the afternoon
A dog barks—well, arf! you pull the cord attached to the monastery
Bell that rings utterly somewhere else
Perhaps the cord is ringing
And you are a Russian
In some hideously small town
Or worst of all
You're listening to the story behind the bell
A history whose rugged but removed features
Resemble those of the sandwich man
Not the one that wandered off into the swamp
Cuffs filled with wind
And was never seen again
But this new one who overestimates his duty by teaching
School in a place that has as students
At best only a bunch of heavily panting dogs
Seated in rows of wooden and iron desks linked
Like slaves on a dismal galley, the Ship of Genius
Sailing for some points known and a few unknown
Caring little about either, huffing away
Toward the horizon destroyed by other students . . . *estudianti*

One of these others, the head, is in fact the Infanta,
In reality only a very intelligent little girl
But beyond the immense corrugated brook we know of as this earth
Covered with raving, a constellation in the shape of a bullet—
She always did love the sound of a ricochet—and I too
Can hear it often, at night, before I go to sleep
In my nose

In Spain, ah
In Spain there are the prune fields and the dark
Beauty of a prune now lowers a shade
Past the sewing machine, over which blow long, regular waves of dust
      particles
In one of which a medium-sized boy in white sandals is peddling up to
Offer you a worried rose

Rose . . . but I know nothing of this rose
Although I will draw it for you in words if you wish
Clockwise beginning at noon on the outer rim
On the first petal is a cave and the second a squiggle
The third a proper noun or else a common noun beginning a sentence
Or perhaps a noun capitalized for no reason at all, for God's sake!

Japan! Penitentiary!
That's what we want!
To move and dance
With strangers, people we don't know
With lines and circles going through us
Who are the landscape

Whose clouds are really toots from the nearby factory
I love so much, the steam factory, making steam
For people to fall down on and permit their bodies to vibrate
Occasionally a straw hat is flung through the factory window
And sails spinning into the water

It is night

A dog barks outside the window
Either that or the window's silent in the dog
—You'll say I'm playing the overture
And finale off against each other, after all
There's no other way to locate the middle,
Which is more elusive than it might seem:
The fifty yard line does escape
The gridiron, extending itself through
Both grandstands, through you and me, plus
A parking lot now indistinguishable from the fog, backyards, dreams,
      washing . . .

And the large peanut that has come to stand for something beautiful and
    intelligent
In short, civilization.
"No so!" says a man in striped pants wheeled in out of the moonlight.
"You think this only because you associate this object with yourselves . . .
    which is okay by me . . . ."
He was wheeled out and chucked over the balcony
Into the magnolia bushes.

At dawn, I find one other example, though nearly driven away
By the dust on it:
You are, say, six feet tall
Or six feet long,
In the first instance you are an active human being other than a baby
In the second you are either a very large baby or
A corpse or perhaps a bed-ridden invalid or
Two yardsticks placed end to end. What your six feet
Would be were you tilted at a 45 degree angle
I do not know
Doubtless a census taker's nightmare, in which bent
Horrible monsters jump out and bite him.

The next step is to know that this fuzzy angle is true in your heart
But not to know what happens to it
When it leaves there, flowers gushing out . . . .
It appears in Amsterdam always
City of extension cords
And ladies with boxes of rubber bands and
A truly horrible music washing the streets rushing below the pigeons
That now seem to be following him as sure as iron
Follows a crook

I don't think I can stand it! the birds
Are swooping down in and out of a large design yes!
A police car is pulling itself together
In the skies, its headlights on now
Bearing down on the sandwich man, still reading,
Whose next step puts him behind
Us as we turn ourselves around to see his other board
And the horrible license plate on it

Le mouvement de César Franck

On a laissé des raisins secs

Quelle que soit la raison, le spectacle qu'ils présentent est digne
        d'admiration

En même temps, dans les jardins, le soir commence

En effet, d'immenses forêts couvrent déjà la contrée

Les mains de la reine passaient successivement sur diverses seigneurs

A gauche de l'avenue d'Iéna

On change de pantalons. Très bien. Pour moi

Si je penche vers le palais de l'Industrie

Le soleil tombé derrière des tours roses et blanches, j'y

Goute une paix profonde.

Un kiosque à musique

S'éleva

Loin du mouvement de César Franck   où je me promène

Auteur d'une histoire féconde

En triangles d'asphalte

Around Paris

Everything in Paris is round.
First is the city itself
Intersected by an arc—
Which is a division of a circle—
Which is the Seine.
Then the well-known spokes
Around the Arch of Triumph.
The cafe table tops are round as well
As the coasters (and many of the ash trays)
That sit upon them.
Looking up, the cafes themselves
Their names at least, are round.
Over there for instance is La Ronde, La Coupole, Le Dôme, La Rotonde
And others.
Only the beautiful Closerie des Lilas escapes our classification
And still remains in Paris.
The lilac, is it round?
People here do a lot of sitting around
As in the Luxembourg Gardens
Where the toy sailboats go round the artificial pond.
They do this.
Last but not least—and how natural!
Are the paintings of Robert Delaunay
Called *The Windows*
In which Paris is seen
As lots of circles.

The Statue of a Libertine

I've chosen this title not only because I like it
But also because it embodies the kind of miniature grandness
A toy instrument has, or powerful dwarf, half sinister
Half pleasure and unexplained

Now I address the statue

Lips that were once as volatile
As similes spoken by an insane person
Who resembled the carving of an irrational human being
But one endowed with such sweetness the pockets are
Blown to bits through their emptiness,

There is no margin of doubt to this reverse
Power, it moves back immediately, a Leonardo's square
You start back from—it extends a confusing,
Buffered metric scale of being
Toward the deep green velvet
That makes sleep possible
Near the gravel smitten with the gloam's evocative power—
These unintentionally horrible memories cling like peaches to the walls
Of the streets where stilettos whiz swiftly toward an incorrect mansion,
    probably

Not very pleasant thoughts
MOVE TOO QUICKLY

What's happening is that we're pawning especially
The vegetation
                    Watch it   There was a first light of print
Then suddenly my view of things
Either enlarges or contracts incredibly
And all I can see is the two of us, you
With your long dark hair, me looking at your hair against the screen
In this small kitchen with its yellow and white curtains
Shot into place with light
And everything else is gone forever
If it does nothing else, this feeling, at least

It relieves my temporal worries
And then it dawns on you: you're looking at the background
For every painting you've ever seen!
It's a kitchen exactly like this one
Containing the orange juice and two dozen eggs
And the coffee pot, the electric
One Tessie and I posed on either side of just before our trip to Rome
We went flying over Rome in a giant aspirin
We didn't see much but were free from headache
(This on a postcard home)
Moving up I thought I'd have the aspirin turn to powder
Which would fall on the city—the echo
I didn't answer because not answering is one of the luxuries
We have here, if we have a phone . . . .
But enough of this, my head

The sun is now going up and down so fast I can hardly keep track of what
day today is—it's the next day, in fact, though it shouldn't be: I'm wearing
the same clothes, smoking the same cigarette, the temperature is the
cigarette. There is less darkness outside, though;

Unfortunately, I can't seem to fit it into any reasonable sequence—
                    one hundred fashionable yachts burning
Remind me of a Blaise Cendrars poem about yachts
I translated in Paris
A few minutes before seeing a young girl break
Down and cry in the Boulevard St-Germain. Thomas Hardy
Was with her but didn't seem to notice she was sobbing horribly and
I felt like pushing both of them into the traffic light
My bus had stopped at

2

Higher up, the wrist assumes a puffiness
Not unlike a pajama leg stuffed with hundred dollar bills
But a dramatic resolution is passed
Into the extended index finger whose rushing
Detonates the very tip

The Farmer's Head

At that instant there came a crash more terrific than any that had preceded it, and the whole place glared with intense light. Everyone was momentarily stunned, and when they recovered their senses, Ernest, looking toward the farmhouse, saw a sheet of flame coming from the farmer's head.

"Fire! Fire!" she shouted. "Your head is afire! It's been struck by lightning!"

"By gum! So it has!" yelled the farmer. "It's blazing!"

He was rapidly shouting this as he ran from the barn.

Tone Arm

The clouds go rolling over
The rooftops of the 17th
18th or 19th century buildings—
They are really rolling

You people of the future
How I hate you
You are alive and I'm not
I don't care whether you read my poetry or not

I

The diamond is real—
See how it cusses over the pheasant
A kind of test lad
Who kicked the elevated man on the bag of light
When just ahead a kind of gold foil geometry
Was spread across a time lapse of London

The results of that experiment came later
Since now you know its diction
Just up here come here

The thin family will die out
When the swans on the ornamental lake
Are signalled
By the French Revolution

Sentence the tattered bucket spinning of the tree

What's all this talk about
Law and order
I wish you would go stick your head up your own butt
As well as your hands, feet, midriff, and other parts
I'm sick of you you turd-faced queer

Well

This town ain't very big at sundown
And the other Henry is approaching
The dusky ski
Which is penetrating your heart at this moment

For what is art but a bauble
On the breast of Time
Or the lady that gives you the time

I'd like to cough on the breast
Of the lady who gives me the time
Arta longa vita brevis

It's a codpiece that I brought along this here vitamin boat
Where you and I
The two of us
Can dilly and dally the whole day through
With naught a thought
But of me and of you
Trouble is
You are a sullen dart

I warned you
You should never have come
But now that you're here I may as well tell you everything
About the orb
A man saw a ball of gold

Later

What is this anyway
But a sort of alchemy of the mouse
Who enters and exits from
His little house

New York, March 8 (RP)—
This will be man's greatest accomplishment
Hand in the old night

up the de Kooning

Whose sullen felicitation now emits
A sort of deafening knob
You turn to get to an "in"
Sign

I salute you, jigsaw critters of the Northwest
But please leave this wafer to another
Dram in the presence of a craw

After a fashion
All breathed easier
Through their own noses
Your nose for instance

I've seen many a ruble in my day
But none so fugitive as this one
You have offered me
As a consolation for being the local
Anesthetic of "I warned you, Brett"

You may wish to lock me out of your life forever
Or to live as a lock lives
On the bean of understanding
A mole's destruction of the weathery facts
We all pretend are true—
By the way, signore, they are all true

By the sea
I remember you when I met you
There by the stately sea, the sea
That is both stately and wholly of itself
Your wings resembled arms
Your beak was as if a woman's mouth
Or a man's that resembled an entire woman
Now I understand that you were a man
Dressed as a bird
One wishes to Ernst upon
To feel the nitrogen and mustard guts
                          . . . . ah!
Your muscles are bands of steel! and your beak

Emits a country-and-western-style song

Go away, glib cur
You were not made for poesy
You aspire, how shall I say, too much?

Token

2

I used to know a song about a hamper
It went
"On a large sock, O . . . ."

The rind of Borneo
Is absolutely zero zero
An etude!

Adjourn the cup is pure

Is it perfect if I rip off your sandals
And bring them to you

A dress retreating
Through a forest fire makes another whole sense

Unfortunately and I'm sorry
I forgot the star of the show
I can see it all now

3

Some showdowns are shaping up   the crude limbs of history
And if the definitions are just   a bunch of shit
Step the other way   deftly!
Avoiding the good car

I was just walking in the street in a short-sleeve shirt
This man passes me going the other way
He was going the other way!

Everything
Needs an intermission
Since in these days here and there
There's not much
One can get many little pleasures from

Wood
Fire   Not that I mind going up
Air   In this ace of hearts
Water

He pulled out his giant prick etc.

He?
Who?
Who did?

Some people came to visit me in prison
They said I was going to pieces
But the person they came to be
Took the rest of the stickers away   *(He hands them to her.)*

I suppose we're worth more these days
Pulling out our giant pricks
My friend Joe Brainard wants to sell his body to a medical school

I feel the whole world shaking
Something must be going on
One never knew, dear, oh dear
The shortness of your answers
Would contribute to this sergeant feeling of sadness
That tugs at my ears
On the clean spring days that are going on around me
My mother, my father, and my friends

4

Let's take a string quartet
Playing one of Beethoven's compositions
We may explain it as the scratching
Of a horse's hair against a cat's gut;
Or we may explain it as the mind
Of a genius soaring up to an infinite
Horse's hair scratching against an infinite cat's gut

5

Hasten the chinchilla
For tonight you die

Only a clever ruse extends the wastebasket
Wise men are said to keep
The weather makes no difference is pure information
Rain banging the toes

6

A red car rolls out.
You are the closely pursued prey of a pack of cards,
Or a parcel of fish.
You are, in fact, a slip
Of the tongue drifting to the point of no return.
But you do return this time
As a child trampled by a rabbit.
A red hat burns in the feces about
Which you are led towards an object
Made of ropes and spikes—an instrument.
And you are also the one who lies thirsting near
The edge of the cog, yet cannot reach it with your mouth
Then you hit the dust off the record
Changing everything.

7

What modern poetry needs
Is a good beating
It is the love call of the gorilla
And a knob is born stunningly

On the affirmative plaza
Huge crowds affirm
An affirming machine

There is indeed money in the tummy
Though wisecracks split the ocean
Throwing up a bad leather pellet
You reach for a vegetable
The train is accountably wrecking
But I know
I'll never bring back that awful stick again
To beat you mercifully
Grandma

8

In its own little place near the obviously phony barn
The spirit evaporates like wise cows before a farmer
In the dawn decorated with mist
Warming up
The day's delicate experiences
Death waits at the end of the trail
And he's boss
O who will lay him out with a good right cross
(Religion, do your part)

I wish (toot toot) to eat it and make beautiful music
Together sometime but not right now
You can have your old city environment, though
With its words on boulevards
I want to walk on a wounded leg in fine weather

9

One makes mistakes in order to appear
Before the human race does

Another poop scene: the last
We see of you
Is this pathetic little figure selling olives

Why do you attack the door, aggressive penny?
Because the scissors you left behind
Snip narcotically at a small thing in a cup

Or
The painter's name was interesting—to be precise,
Rather interesting.

10

You have a lovely name-calling instinct
Though some say you stink
Or so you think
Ted to the high heavens
For even the gravest accents trip occasionally
Through fields of wheat, slaw, and a third
Where desolation's grape snuggles closer to
Desolation's other grapes, forming
An excellent, a piercing arrangement

As they do
So do we
These squeeks emerge from scissor-holes
Causing a gentle motion in the eardrums

No, I have nothing to declare
But your country is beautiful
It wishes to stay here

Poinsettia ravages automobile

Subjecting it to summer's gentle torture

The taxi is beautiful because it is open at all hours
Said George Washington Carver
Whose head shall be separated from his body forever more
He went to Chicago in a taxi
Not the Chicago of Sandburg
But the Chicago of tissue and how to get there
Am I disturbing you?
It's wonderful, splendid!
To put one's foot in a Wednesday night rape
You see I am bored
In fact, I am short of money
Here comes winter's dim claw (balance)

     II

Batten down the hatches boys I'm having an idea!
It was cold, very cold . . . .
(What is a house
But a bunch of hints thrown
In and out a window?
This suggests that history
O infinite hints!
Has sometime in its past
Caught up with itself
Come by itself
Passé
Is now only an imitation of itself
Like a car
Driving toward itself in the rain
Developing its own misty personality
Only to be photographed from behind
As we all eventually are.

In other words a house
I suppose
May as well be a horse's ass
Breaking the visible chains of logic.

12

Outside my window is preparing for the darkness
That broke my mother's heart—
For you kiss a pair of lips only to realize,
Later, that it was a single lip, in fact
The Blarney Stone . . . . You see how lucky you really are
Though the bicycle part is over
The fence first. The size of the buildings
You step over is of no importance
Since the buildings brought their own sky,
One you enjoyed but preferred to run
Like a funny baby into

13

The Jews like to eat
The Italians like to eat
The Irish like to drink
The Germans like to think
The French, they like to swim
And sink and swim
MY ANIMALS

14

For one brings everything to a bear
In a crucial moment
On a silver platter—or better yet
A silver spoon whose engraving tells
Of a future

The bear holds a jerking fish in his dumb paw;
In fact, he is standing on his hind legs, and
Judging from this equally bad drawing,
The legs of other bears as well.
That's what it's always been, hasn't it?
From book to bed to book

With nothing but perfect holes between,
Spaces to be filled in later
Or simply brought out as in invisible ink
As the case may be, as
A hammer is brought down as you move toward the bed
A book in one hand a book in the other
Both feet moving, one then the other.
Yes, something is moving toward the bed
As surely as day and night flip through one another
Like a ball.
What might be
Is of no concern to me—
You see I have neither tooth nor brain in my head,
Which love conspires
To relieve you of.

15

He went for an empty holster.
A short circuit was blamed.
It was a musical score.
Try the packet.
And his pants—that's France.

16

Socrates was a mutt, this is generally not known
But understood at some hilarious fork
For a few years! oh
Then watch the ducks peck at gunpowder on the dental walks
Where we pace so as not to upset the tipping lake

Now the ducks are picketing the island
We can get to
The hills (those hills) pose instead and offer themselves
We climb the hellish peanut
Now the ducks are standing in a white surface

The grassy edges rise to music's flown cough
Now the ducks tear the water's surface off
The telling ducks
The park is moving out
Now the ducks cornered in sunset are really burning up
Now the ducks assault the night they're turning away from

O but we could throw down sects
And step on it

17

Sir
Will you please keep going to the bathroom you do it magnificently
Which reminds me
Of this place, this time, you and me
We're back!
We are eating terrific amounts of food
Food food
So we can go to the bathroom good good good

You're weak I'm not
Your
Energy gone down someone else's cheek's rosy sheet
I'm quite comfortable here
In my motorized chair
That was crated by mistake
Those tears could take you miles up
To the rosy heavens we thought so wonderful just a little while ago
Don't I know it

I can't help it Louis, Louis Pasteur
Deft chemist of manure
It's back again that pastille you hated so

18

The genitals run amock

Sliding in and out and around one another
And here I have two beautiful young girls in this room
Both of whom I am going to fuck unmercifully
These girls that skim along a beach of money

Let's say we look
Into this box and
See two ladies talking
With one another. Each
Is standing on a beach.
The lady on the left . . . .

Several peaceful girls come running down the beach
But the letters they are fly away
Like gentle, harmless farts

Those girls I spoke of there
Were hit only here and there
With bright patches of color
They had no bodies
Please do not think of them as the products of a vivid imagination

Right now I just happen to be looking at the Atlantic Ocean
Or at least a part of it
Please to box with me on the beach?

The white pellet passes under the monster
Decorating the fence
Down the fence goes the pellet
Then becomes the pellet of distance
Which is what it always was anyway

Old kinds of geometry are strafing the beach
In search of this famous belly
Perhaps it is the pellet they are searching for
Or the hole made in the sky
By the pellet bye and bye

If I had the world's great grease extinct beside me now
I could at last kill

The people who go out and drop carelessly into the holes
Of the white pinball machine
They tally, yes
But without the ho!
And when you add up the scores
Generosity erases them
After all

19

In guarded spasms you broke the ruler
Vanishing 7
Good heavens! was said

The fact broke the cigarette too
And that mad us
Or the other version of the clink at Columbia University

The clink that falls fiery off the bridge
Over the large canyon
The climate that day was contest though
Crowds disperse. Girls bleed in the great calm

20

You select something small like a pimple
And quick as a wink that's all there is
In a world of moles, pores, hairs and other
Indications are made
Who made them?
Not you, certainly, but the lonely pimple
On its journey to the tip of the nose
Which is its destiny

The blemish you see
is a stage unto itself
And also around itself
One on which you perform

For you are smaller than the smallest pimple
When smoke goes rushing over the vase

When the vase goes rushing over the ocean
I'll be rushing with it
Toward native lands
To take a shower along with me
Dismantling the atmosphere with my hands

21

Sings

When the cows and the leaves begin to fall
They fall like falsehood

Just as coffee comes from the brains
Well-behaved elephants pass

Sandpaper toughens the holes
The dialogues of Plato rage in the pre-dawn

The wind shows off
The cows fall again

The bus goes pitching over Kansas
Joe is reading
I am asleep

I wired the violets

*

A contact lens drifts above the cervix
And it's not a bad idea

You work in a highly visible bowl

22

"I'm coaching in the orange groves
Near the snow fields of my heart"
Is an example of a kind of poetry
I wish to discuss here. It is not
Simply great poetry nor is it simply
Great sentiment, it is both.

23

You go on as a taxicab keeping still to this music
Me, I do my homework

Hashish go
Under your dress . . . at the dining room table
All suspect.
              And you tsk
The Pied Piper, 6 foot 4.

—Classic January black—
Prince P. broke the light on the porch
Where used to run and play the glass figure
That is no more!

24

I am shaving in the distance
The nights come and pass by
Come and pass by
There is a tremendous nature here
Where I am
A shirt is here, too

The Haunted House

Put a coin on the doorstep. Gears begin
to whirr—light above door flashes.

Slowly the door swings open. A ghostly
figure steals out—and covers the coin.

Suddenly the ghost takes the coin and
fades back into the house.

Remembrance of Things Past

I'm afraid father's hair is slightly cancelled
In three general areas:
First in the town,
Then the in-between,
And finally the second town.
For it is difficult and not even necessary to decide
Where he is
For he sits enthroned in himself
Before a flowery screen
Reading the completely white newspaper.
Son is playing with a watering can,
A white disc, a sabre, and probably earlier
A blue bag. The sabre is held up in his right hand.
Yes, son, you may play with the sabre
Only please do not disturb me with it in any way,
Or disturb me in any other way either.
I wish to read,
To read this newspaper,
Or . . . do I wish to sleep?
Now that father has gone to sleep
Faster than any human ever,
I may show you, O observer!
This disc which is a tambourine,
I may use my left hand to strike this match,
Apply it to and set fire to the newspaper.
The blue bag . . . .
Ah! you little son of a bitch,
Down before me as you are on one knee,
Kneeling, what have you done?
You've set fire to my newspaper,
Woke me up, bothered me in a vicious manner,
And generally done something you shouldn't have.
The blue bag . . . .
Must I open my arms and tilt my head forgivingly
When you say you will never do it again?
You see out of the corner of your eye

That my newspaper has stopped burning
And lies where I dropped it, half covering the blue bag
Near the tambourine,
Far from the cancellation which has become
In the manner of a painting a work of art.

December

I will sleep
in my little cup

Poem for Joan Inglis on Her Birthday

As he stood saying goodbye
to the small, empty stage
on which he had played
the happiest scene of his life,
he noticed that
the mirror was reflecting
the counter, and that
a thin streak of light showed at the top
of the door behind it. At
the same moment the wind
swept down the street again,
ripping a board
from the wall across the way,
rising
to hurricane violence
as it howled past
and in the mirror he saw the door
behind the counter burst its catch
and swing inwards,
revealing the widening oblong of the inner room,
the bedpost with a bright blue coat and a tie
hanging over it, the corner
of the dressing-table and a
small, darkly shaded lamp.

Joe Brainard's Painting *Bingo*

I suffer when I sit next to Joe Brainard's painting *Bingo*

I could have made that line into a whole stanza

I suffer
When I sit
Next to Joe
Brainard's painting
Bingo

Or I could change the line arrangement

I suffer when I sit

That sounds like hemorrhoids
I don't know anything about hemorrhoids
Such as if it hurts to sit when you have them
If so I must not have them
Because it doesn't hurt me to sit
I probably sit about 8/15 of my life

Also I don't suffer
When I sit next to Joe Brainard

Actually I don't even suffer
When I sit next to his painting *Bingo*
Or for that matter any of his paintings

In fact I didn't originally say
I suffer when I sit next to Joe Brainard's painting *Bingo*
My wife said it
In response to something I had said
About another painting of his
She had misunderstood what I had said

Wonderful Things

Anne, who are dead   and whom I loved in a rather asinine fashion
         I think of you often

    buveur de l'opium chaste et doux
                                Yes I think of you
   with very little in mind

   as if I had become a helpless moron

               Watching zany chirping birds

       That inhabit the air

And often ride our radio waves

So I've been sleeping lately with no clothes on
The floor   which is very early   considering the floor
Is made of birds and they are flying and I am
Upsidedown and ain't it great to be great!!

Seriously I have this mental (smuh) illness

                      which causes me to do things

                            on and away

Straight for the edge

Of a manicured fingernail
Where it is deep and dark   and green   and silent

Where I may go at will
And sit down and tap

My forehead against the sunset

Where he takes off the uniform
And we see he is God

God get out of here

And he runs off chirping and chuckling into his hand

And that is a wonderful thing

. . . a tuba that is a meadowful of bluebells
is a wonderful thing

and that's what I want to do

Tell you wonderful things

Reading Reverdy

The wind that went through the head left it plural.

*

The half-erased words on the wall of bread.

*

Someone is grinding the color of ears.

*

She looks like and at her.

*

A child draws a man and the earth
Is covered with snow.

*

He comes down out of the night
When the hills fall.

*

The line part of you goes out to infinity.

*

I get up on top of an inhuman voice.

Strawberries in Mexico

At 14th Street and First Avenue
Is a bank and in the bank the sexiest teller of all time
Next to her the greatest thing about today
Is today itself
Through which I go up
To buy books

They float by under a bluer sky
The girls uptown
Quiet, pampered
The sum of all that's terrible in women
And much of the best

And the old men go by holding small packages
In a trance
So rich even *they* can't believe it

I think it's a red, white, and blue letter day for them too
You see, Con Ed's smokestacks *are* beautiful
The way Queens is
And horses: from a pleasant distance

Or a fleet of turkeys
Stuffed in a spotless window
In two days they'll be sweating in ovens
Thinking, "How did I ever get in a fix like this?"

Light pouring over buildings far away

Up here when someone shouts "Hey!"
In the street you know that they aren't going to kill you
They're yelling to a friend of theirs named Hey
John David Hey, perhaps
And the garbage goes out
In big white billowy plastic bags tied at the top
And even the people go out in them

Some are waiting now
At the bus stop (for a nonexistent bus)
And I thought it was garbage!
It's so pretty!

If you're classless or modern
You can have fun by
Walking into a high-class antique store
So the stately old snob at the desk will ask
In eternity
"You're going where?"
You get to answer, "Up."

I like these old pricks
If you have an extra hair in the breeze
Their eyes pop out
And then recede way back
As if to say, "That person is on . . . dope!"
They're very correct

But they're not in my shoes
In front of a Dubuffet a circus that shines through
A window in a bright all-yellow building
The window is my eye
And Frank O'Hara is the building
I'm thinking about him like mad today
(As anyone familiar with his poetry will tell)
And about the way Madison Avenue really
Does go to heaven
And turns around and comes back, disappointed

Because up here you can look down on the janitor
Or pity him
And rent a cloud-colored Bentley and
Architecture's so wonderful!
Why don't I notice it more often?
And the young girls and boys but especially the young girls
Are drifting away from school
In blue and white wool
Wrapped in fur

Are they French? They're speaking French!
And they aren't looking for things to throw
Skirts sliding up the legs of girls who can't keep from grinning
Under beautiful soft brown American eyes
At the whole world
Which includes their plain Jane girlfriends
She even smiled at me!
I have about as much chance of fucking her as the girl at the bank
But I stride along, a terrifying god
Raunchy
A little one-day-old beard
And good grief I really did forget to brush my teeth this morning
They're turning red with embarrassment
Or is that blood
I've been drinking—I ordered a black coffee
Miss

And then a black policeman comes in
Unbuttoning his uniform at the warmish soda fountain
While I pull the fleece over my teeth
And stare innocently at the books I've bought
One a book with a drawing
By Apollinaire called *Les Fraises au Mexique*
Strawberries in Mexico
But when I open the book to that page
It's just a very blue sky I'm looking at

Detach, Invading

Oh humming all and
Then a something from above came rooting
And tooting onto the sprayers
Profaning in the console morning
Of the pointing afternoon
Back to dawn by police word to sprinkle it
Over the lotions that ever change
On locks
Of German, room, and perforate
To sprinkle I say
On the grinding slot of rye
And the bandage that falls down
On the slots as they exude their gas
And the rabbit lingers that pushes it

To blot the lumber
Like a gradually hard mode
All bring and forehead in the starry grab
That pulverizes
And its slivers
Off bending down the thrown gulp
In funny threes
So the old fat flies toward the brain
And a dent on brilliance

The large pig at which the intense cones beat
Wishes O you and O me
O cough release! a rosy bar
Whose mist rarifies even the strokers
Where to go
Strapping, apricot

Ron Padgett is a poet. He always has been a poet and he always will be a poet. I don't know how a poet becomes a poet. And I don't think anyone else does either. It is something deep and mysterious inside of a person that cannot be explained. It is something that no one understands. I asked Ron Padgett once how it came about that he was a poet, and he said, "I don't know. It is something deep and mysterious inside of me that cannot be explained."

—Joe Brainard